How Artists See
ANIMALS
Mammal Fish Bird Reptile

Colleen Carroll

ABBEVILLE KIDS
A DIVISION OF ABBEVILLE PUBLISHING GROUP
New York London

"Painters understand nature and love her and teach us to see her."

—VINCENT VAN GOGH

This book is dedicated to my nephews, Charles and Benjamin, and to my niece, Theresa, three great kids and friends of animals.

I'd like to thank the many people who helped make this book happen, especially Jackie Decter, Ed Decter, Colleen Mohyde, and as always, my husband, Mitch Semel.

—COLLEEN CARROLL

JACKET AND COVER FRONT: Franz Marc, *The Yellow Cow,* 1911 (see also pages 6 and 7).
JACKET AND COVER BACK, LEFT: Roy Lichtenstein, *Goldfish Bowl, II,* 1978 (see also pages 14 and 15); RIGHT: John James Audubon, *American Flamingo,* 1838 (see also pages 20 and 21).
JACKET BACK, BOTTOM: Robert Jew, *Lizard Head* (detail), 1994 (see also pages 32 and 33).

EDITOR: Jacqueline Decter
DESIGNER: Patricia Fabricant
PRODUCTION EDITOR: Abigail Asher
PRODUCTION MANAGER: Lou Bilka

 The text of this book was set in Stempel Schneidler. Printed and bound in China.

First library edition
10 9 8

ISBN-13: 978-0-7892-0475-2
ISBN-10: 0-7892-0475-4

Library of Congress Cataloging-in-Publication Data
Carroll, Colleen.
Animals : mammal, fish, bird, reptile / Colleen Carroll.
p. cm. — (How artists see, ISSN 1083-821X)
Includes bibliographical references.
Summary: Examines how different kinds of animals have been depicted in works of art from different time periods and places.
ISBN 0-7892-0059-7;
0-7892-0475-4 (library edition)
1. Animals in art—Juvenile literature. [1. Animals in art. 2. Art appreciation.] I. Title. II. Series: Carroll, Colleen. How artists see.
N7668.C29 1996
701'.01—dc20 95-25795

For bulk and premium sales and for text adoption procedures, write to Customer Service Manager, Abbeville Press, 137 Varick Street, New York, NY 10013, or call 1-800-ARTBOOK.

Visit Abbeville Press online at www.abbeville.com.

CONTENTS

MAMMAL

GROUP OF STAGS

Lascaux Caves, France

Did you know that the very first paintings are pictures of animals? Thousands of years ago, prehistoric artists made paintings of bison, lions, horses, and many other kinds of animals on cave walls. (Paper and canvas had yet to be invented). Some of the animals you're about to see will be familiar to you, and others will be strange and exotic. Now keep reading to discover many of the ways that artists see animals.

You probably recognize the animals in this picture. What details help you to tell? The painting is made in a very simple way, with only a few dark lines to show the animals' shapes. The herd seems to be moving across the wall. Maybe they're looking for food, or maybe they're running away from a hunter. Where do you think they might be going? If you use your imagination, you might be able to hear their hooves as they move. What do they sound like to you?

MAMMAL

THE YELLOW COW

by Franz Marc

Chances are you've never seen a cow like this before. Of course, the artist who made this painting hadn't either, except in his imagination. This extraordinary cow leaps through a landscape filled with brilliant colors that seem to come from a dream. How many colors can you find? What words would you use to describe this colorful cow?

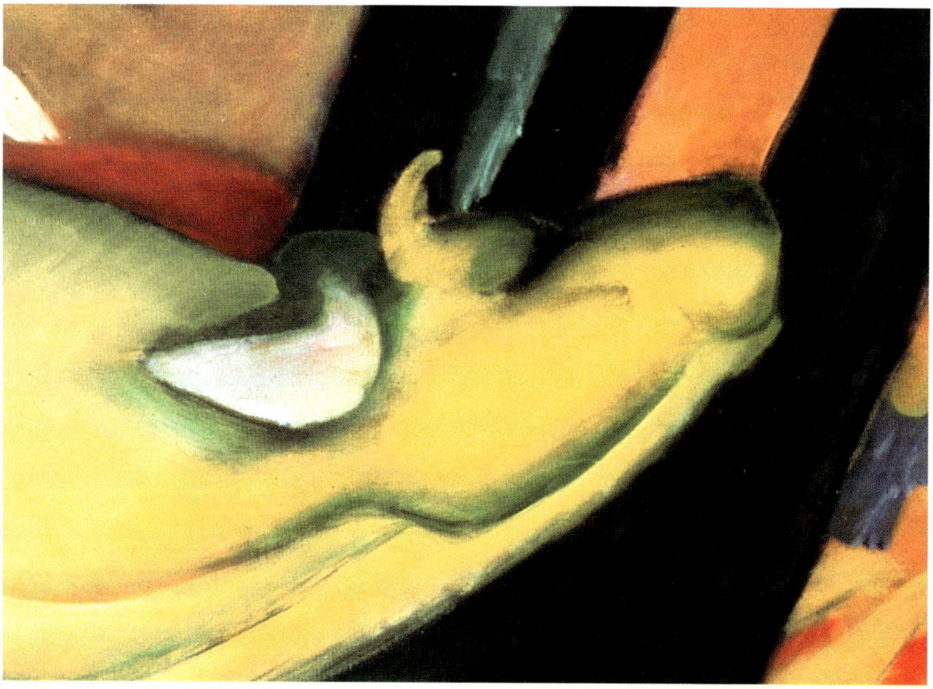

Everyone knows that real cows aren't yellow and blue, but artists sometimes change the way things really look to express a feeling or to make you look at familiar things in a new way. Try to imagine this same picture with a black and white cow and a green countryside. How would realistic colors change the feeling of the painting? Do you think it would be as much fun to look at?

TIGER BY A TORRENT

by Kishi Ganku

No one would mistake this tiger, with its deep orange coat, black stripes, and bright green eyes, for any other animal. The artist drew the tiger in action as it gingerly steps down a rocky path along a stream of rushing water. It rests its great weight on a front paw and twists its body toward something on the other side of the stream. What do you think it sees? Do you think it will be able to cross the water safely?

Look closely at the tiger's thick, velvety coat. The artist drew hundreds of tiny lines to make the texture look so realistic. What other realistic details can you find? The big cat bares its long, white fangs and glares off into the distance. Can you snarl like this ferocious, beautiful animal?

MAMMAL

THE WATER HOLE

by N. C. Wyeth

When you want a drink at a water fountain, you probably have to stand in a line. These buffalo are doing just that as they make their way over hills and down paths to a refreshing water hole. Do they seem to be rushing quickly toward the water or moving at a leisurely pace?

There are many lines of animals in this picture. Starting with the biggest buffalo, trace your finger over each of

the lines. You may notice that the animals get smaller and lighter until they become tiny spots of gray paint. Artists do this to create a feeling of wide, open space that reaches far into the distance. The smallest buffalo in the background still has a lot of ground to cover. How thirsty would you be if you had to walk this far for a drink of water?

THE GOLDFISH BOWL

by Henri Matisse

You've probably seen these fish before. Well, not these exact fish, but fish like them. They're goldfish, of course. You may even have your very own goldfish bowl at home or at school. These special goldfish swim in a bowl surrounded by vivid colors and bold patterns. Some of the patterns are made of shapes that look like fish. Point to all the fish-shaped objects you can find. Now look at the blurry patches of orange floating at the top of the bowl. What do you think they are?

GOLDFISH BOWL, II

by Roy Lichtenstein

Here's another bowl of goldfish made by a different artist. It has many things in common with the picture you just saw, but the artists have created two very different works of art. First, this artwork is a sculpture made from metal. The other is a painting. Second, these fish are darker and have heavy black outlines. What other similarities and differences can you find? Which fish look more real to you?

Sometimes artists get ideas by looking at the works of other artists whom they respect and admire. Then they add their own unique style to make the work new and original. Which style do you prefer?

THE FISH

by Alexander Calder

Artists often use materials in very clever ways. This sculpture is made with lots of odds and ends, such as broken glass, buttons, beads, and stones—the kinds of things that most people would throw away. Some of the pieces were made by hand, like the spiral object in the fish's tail. What other unusual materials can you find? These bits and

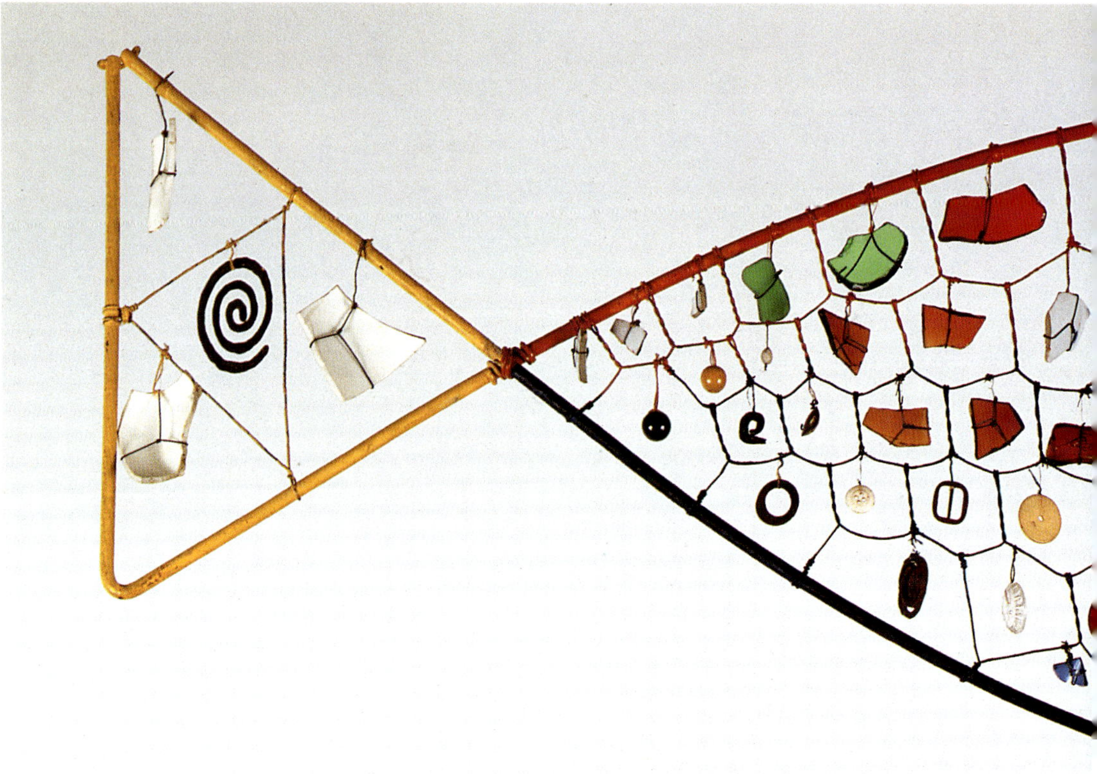

pieces help you to imagine the texture of a fish's scales. Are they smooth and slippery or rough and sharp? How is the round, green glass similar to a fish's eye?

This type of sculpture, called a mobile, hangs from the ceiling in a museum and seems to "swim" through the air. Imagine the fish moving through the water with its mouth agape. Do you think it's hungry? How many tiny fish do you think it could swallow at once?

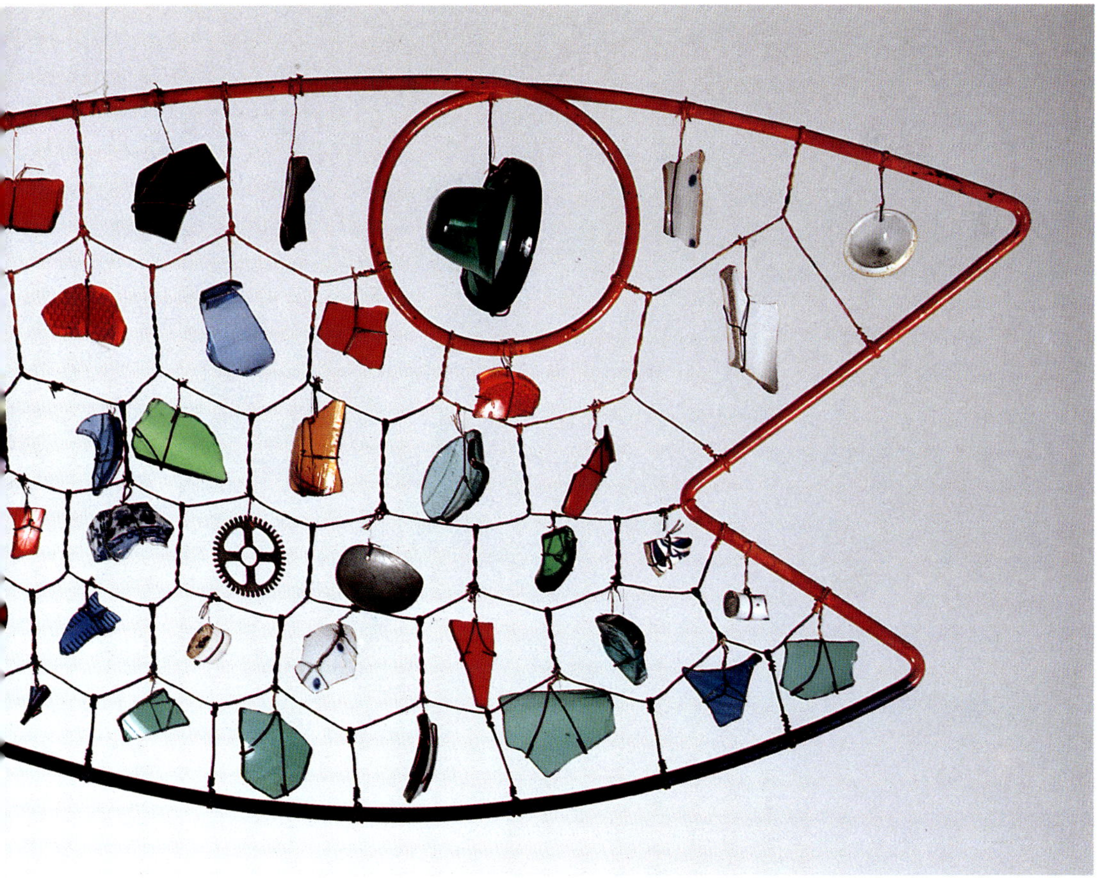

FISH MAGIC

by Paul Klee

There's something fishy going on here. The artist has created a mysterious underwater world for a strange school of fish. How many fish can you spot? Some of the things in the picture you might expect to see in the water, such as divers, flowers, and seaweed. But other things don't seem to belong underwater. Can you find them?

Why do you think the artist named this painting *Fish Magic?* With their bright colors against a black background, these bizarre creatures seem to glow in the dark. Would you want to swim in this eerie aquarium?

BIRD

AMERICAN FLAMINGO

by John James Audubon

This flamingo is really in the pink. The artist who made the picture spent most of his life watching all kinds of birds and drawing them in their natural environments. Can you tell where home is for these birds? The big flamingo in the foreground bends its spindly legs and lowers its head to the water. Trace your finger along its curving neck. What do you think the bird is doing in this funny position?

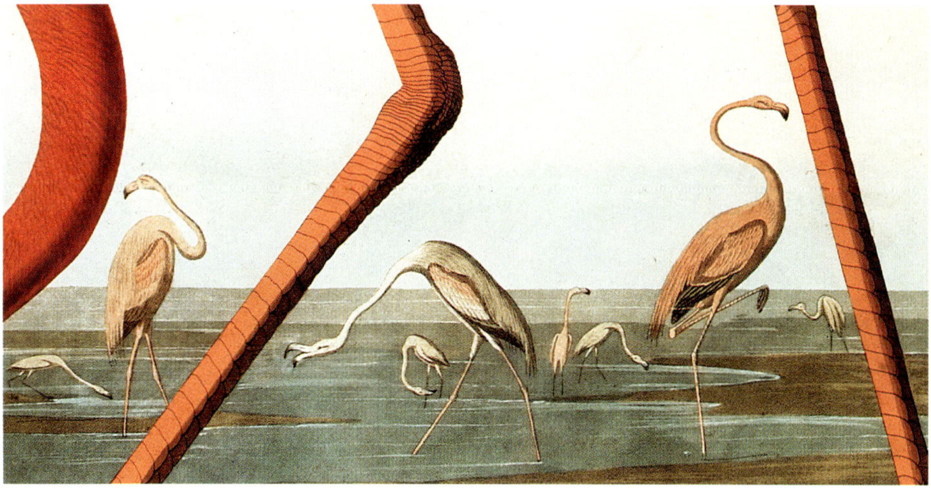

You may have noticed the small sketches at the top of the picture. Sometimes artists make studies as a way of practicing before making a final picture. What parts of the bird's body do you see in these drawings? Can you find them on the big bird?

Drawn from Nature by J. J. Audubon, F.R.S. F.L.S.
Engraved, Printed and Coloured by Robt. Havell 1838
1. Profile view of Bill at its greatest extension.
2. Superior front view of upper Mandible.
3. Interior front view of upper Mandible.
4. Inferior front view of lower Mandible.
5. Interior front view of lower Mandible with the Tongue in
American Flamingo.
PHŒNICOPTERUS RUBER, Linn.
Old Male
6. Profile view of Tongue.
7. Superior front view of Tongue.
8. Inferior front view of Tongue.
9. Perpendicular front view of the foot, fully expanded

BIRD

WHEATFIELD WITH CROWS

by Vincent Van Gogh

Where are the birds in this picture? If you noticed the black lines that look like flapping wings, you've found them. With just a few simple lines, the artist created a whole flock of crows. Have you ever drawn birds this way before?

Some of the larger birds seem to be very close, while the smaller ones seem so far away that their shapes blend into the sky. Perhaps they've flown a great distance to reach the wheat field, or maybe they're flying away to a different place. Do you think the crows are coming or going? What sounds might you hear if you were standing in this field?

BIRD IN SPACE

by Constantin Brancusi

Although you might not believe it, this graceful sculpture is of a bird. It may not look like a real bird, but that wasn't what the artist was trying to do. Instead, he was trying to capture the feeling of a bird in flight. Trace your finger up from the bottom of the sculpture and beyond the pointed tip. How does the curved shape help you imagine a bird soaring through the air?

Have you ever wondered to yourself how it would feel to fly like a bird? Even though this sculpture looks very simple, the artist had to think carefully about what birds look like to capture the feeling of flight. What parts of a bird's body do you think he was imagining as he created this work of art? Was it the wing or the tail? Maybe it was the beak. Perhaps it was a combination of many things. If you were making a sculpture of a bird, what parts would you choose?

BLACK BIRD OVER SNOW-COVERED RED HILLS

by Georgia O'Keeffe

Have you ever pretended to fly like a bird? Here's another artist who's shown the beauty of a bird in flight, but she's done it in a more realistic way. If you could hitch a ride on the back of this sleek, painted blackbird, what would you see on the ground below?

This artist, too, used gently curving lines to make this graceful bird and to help you imagine what it must feel like to fly. The bird soars through a wide, open sky with extended wings. Move your finger over the lines of its body. Now trace these same lines through the air with your arms, as if you were a bird gliding over these snowy hills.

THE SNAKE CHARMER

by Henri Rousseau

Have you ever seen so many slithering snakes in one picture? How many can you find? You'll have to look carefully to spot them all. This lush jungle landscape is filled with lines and shapes that seem to sway and wriggle, such as the reeds at the water's edge and the striped plants on the right. What other snakelike shapes do you see?

The snake charmer stands very still as she plays her instrument, luring the snakes out of the trees and grasses. The music must be very special to charm so many snakes. Try to imagine the tune she plays. Is it fast or slow? What does it sound like to you?

REPTILE

CROCODILES

by John Singer Sargent

The artist who made this picture thought these reptiles were crocodiles, but they're really a bunch of resting alligators. How many of them can you find? You may not see them all at first, because the artist painted only two of them clearly. The shapes and colors of the other alligators blend into the sandy shore, so your eyes and imagination must fill in the details. Use your finger to outline their shapes. Which parts are the easiest to recognize? Which parts do you have to imagine?

The powerful reptiles look harmless as they bask in the sun along the water's edge. The artist grouped them in a tight circle surrounded by streaks of violet and brown watercolor paint. In some places the colors blend together to make a dark shade of green. Why do you think the artist chose these colors? Do you think the painting would look as mysterious if the artist had used more realistic colors?

REPTILE

LIZARD HEAD

by Robert Jew

This iguana looks so real, it seems as if it might just crawl off its leafy canvas at any moment. Some artists show their subject matter up close so you can see even the smallest details, such as the tiny circles that surround the reptile's eye. Look closely at the picture and study the iguana's face. What other details do you see?

The lizard's skin is an intricate pattern of rounded shapes and bright colors. How many shades of green can you

find? If you could move your finger over its skin, what would the texture feel like? How would it be different from the texture of the green leaves or the frill at the top of its head? Maybe some day you'll be this close to a real iguana and find out for yourself.

伯子逸

FROG ON A LOTUS LEAF

by Hsiang Sheng-mo

Frogs are amphibians, which are distant cousins of reptiles. Can you tell what this plump green frog is trying to do? To discover the answer, just follow its stare. What do you see? The frog is very still and focuses on its prey with great concentration. If this picture could come to life, what do you think would happen next?

This artist, like many in this book, shows animals in their natural environments. Other artists create wondrous settings where their animals swim, run, and play. Some of the animals look very real, and others are fantastic products of the artist's imagination. Now that you've discovered how some artists see animals, use your own unique vision to create a picture of your favorite animal.

NOTE TO PARENTS AND TEACHERS

As an elementary school teacher, I had the opportunity to show my students many examples of great art. I was always amazed by their enthusiastic responses to the colors, shapes, subjects, and fascinating stories of the artists' lives. It wasn't uncommon for us to spend twenty minutes looking at and talking about just one work of art. By asking challenging questions, I prompted the children to examine and think very carefully about the art, and then quite naturally they would begin to ask all sorts of interesting questions of their own. These experiences inspired me to write this book and the other volumes in the *How Artists See* series.

How Artists See is designed to teach children about the world by looking at art, and about art by looking at the world through the eyes of great artists. The books encourage children to look critically, answer—and ask—thought-provoking questions, and form an appreciation and understanding of an artist's vision. Each book is devoted to a single subject so that children can see how different artists have approached and treated the same theme and begin to understand the importance of individual style.

Because I believe that children learn most successfully in an atmosphere of exploration and discovery, I've included questions that encourage them to formulate ideas and responses for themselves. And because people's reactions to art are based on their own personal aesthetic, most of the questions are open-ended and have more than one answer. If you're reading aloud to your children or students, give them ample time to look at each work and formulate a response; it certainly is not necessary to read the whole book in one sitting. Like a good book or movie, art can be enjoyed over and over again, each time with the possibility of revealing something that wasn't seen before.

You may notice that dates and other historical information are not included in the main text. I purposely omitted this information in order to focus on the art and those aspects of the world it illustrates. For children who want to learn more about the artists whose works appear in the book, short biographies are provided at the end, along with suggestions for further reading and a list of museums where you can see additional works by each artist.

After reading *How Artists See Animals,* children can do a wide variety of related activities to extend and reinforce all that they've learned. In addition to the simple activities I've suggested throughout the main text, they can visit a local zoo or wildlife sanctuary to further their appreciation of animals, or create stories about their own pets or favorite animals in the book. Since the examples shown here are just a tiny fraction of the great works of art that feature animals as their subject, children can go on a scavenger hunt through museums and the many wonderful art books in your local library to find other images of animals.

I hope that you and your children or students will enjoy reading and rereading this book and, by looking at many styles of art, discover how artists share with us their unique ways of seeing and depicting our world.

ARTISTS' BIOGRAPHIES

(in order of appearance)

If you'd like to know more about the artists in this book, here's some information to get you started:

CAVE PAINTERS (c. 15,000–10,000 B.C.), *pp. 4–5*

Perhaps the greatest mystery in all of art lies in the prehistoric paintings found on cave walls in what are today the countries of France and Spain. Very little is known about the artists who made these paintings of bulls, horses, deer, and other animals. Some people think the paintings were part of an ancient religion, and others think they were made to bring good luck and strength to hunters. Whatever the reasons, these paintings tell us that people have been making art and expressing themselves in a creative way for over 15,000 years.

FRANZ MARC (1880–1916), *pp. 6–7*

Early in the twentieth century, a small group of painters began to use color in new and unusual ways. One of these painters was Franz Marc. This German artist believed that color was very powerful and could help to express his emotions. Artists who use color to express feelings are called Expressionists. Marc also believed in the spirit, grace, and power of animals. He combined these beliefs to create beautiful paintings of vividly colored animals, such as bright blue horses and the yellow cow seen in this book. Sadly, Franz Marc painted only for a short period of time. He was killed on a battlefield during World War I at the age of thirty-six.

KISHI GANKU (1750–1838), *pp. 8–9*

Kishi Ganku (pronounced *gon-coo*) was a mostly self-taught Japanese painter who lived during the middle of the Yedo Period, a time of great artistic achievement in Japan. As a young man he traveled all over the country and eventually made his home in the city of Kyoto. Like many Japanese artists of the day, Ganku founded his own school of painting, called the Kishi school. He is best known for his realistic and energetic paintings of animals in their natural habitats.

NEWELL CONVERS (N. C.) WYETH (1882–1945), *pp. 10–11*

As a boy growing up on a Massachusetts farm, N. C. Wyeth (pronounced *WHY-ith*) liked to draw pictures of the nature he saw all around him. As a young man, Wyeth traveled to the western United States to see the subjects that interested him most: cowboys, animals, and Native Americans. At age twenty-one he sold a drawing of a cowboy on a bucking bronco to a well-known magazine, and from then on he found great success as an illustrator. He went on to illustrate many classic children's stories, such as *Treasure Island, Robin Hood, The Last of the Mohicans,* and *The Yearling.* Wyeth was also an easel painter, and toward the end of his life he painted many beautiful still lifes and landscapes around his home in Pennsylvania. His son Andrew and his grandson Jamie became artists as well.

HENRI MATISSE (1869–1954), *pp. 12–13*

During his long life, Henri Matisse (pronounced *mah-TIECE*) worked in many different styles. Early in his career he was the leader of a group of painters called the Fauves, which in French means "wild beasts." The Fauves believed that color was the most important element in painting and they used it in bold ways. In one of Matisse's most well-known portraits, he painted his wife's face bright green! His favorite subjects included dancers, still lifes, and interiors of colorful rooms. Late in his life, when he could no longer paint, Matisse made collages out of brightly colored paper, which he called "cut-outs." Along with another artist named Pablo Picasso, Matisse is known as "the father of modern art," because his ideas took art in new directions.

ROY LICHTENSTEIN (1923–1997), *pp. 14–15*

This American painter is known as a "Pop" artist because of his paintings of popular things that people can recognize from everyday life. Lichtenstein (pronounced *LICK-ten-stine*) is most famous for his comic-book-style paintings—pictures that show the bright colors, black outlines, and Benday dots of real newspaper comic strips. He is also known for using this unique style to re-create paintings by other famous artists, such as the sculpture in this book.

ALEXANDER CALDER (1898–1976), *pp. 16–17*

The son and grandson of sculptors, this American artist learned from an early age how to make things. As a young man living in Paris, France, he made his now famous wire *Circus,* complete with movable clowns, animals, and acrobats. He is best known for his mobiles—sculptures made of flat, brightly colored metal shapes that look like objects from nature, such as fish, leaves, or animals. These sculptures are hung from the ceiling with wire and move with the changing air currents. Calder also made large metal sculptures known as stabiles (like the word "stable"). These stabiles, which don't move, are most often found in wide, open spaces, such as city squares and sculpture gardens.

PAUL KLEE (1879–1940), *pp. 18–19*

Can you imagine what it would be like to "take a line for a walk"? That's how this Swiss artist and teacher described his style of painting. Paul Klee (pronounced *clay*) used lines and shapes to create paintings that seem to come from a dreamworld. He loved the way children made drawings, and his own work sometimes resembles children's art. Klee was fond of painting pictures of children, fish, and creatures from his vivid imagination.

JOHN JAMES AUDUBON (1785–1851), *pp. 20–21*

After growing up in Paris, France, Audubon (pronounced *AW-due-bon*) moved to America, where he lived and worked for the rest of his life. Audubon was fascinated with birds, and decided to devote his life to studying and painting them in their natural habitats. He traveled all over the country, searching for as many species as he could find. At first Audubon shot and killed hundreds of birds in order to study them for his paintings, but he came to believe that this practice was wrong and that all people must do their part to protect wildlife. Today, Audubon's bird paintings are collected in a book called *Audubon's Birds of America.*

VINCENT VAN GOGH (1853–1890), *pp. 22–23*

Even though this Dutch artist painted for only seven years, he left behind hundreds of paintings and drawings that are among the world's most famous and beloved artworks. Vincent van Gogh (pronounced *van-GO*) used bright colors and thick brush strokes. He liked to paint outdoors in full sunlight, and often painted two pictures a day. His brother Theo worked for an art dealer and sent Vincent paints and canvas so that he could spend most of his time painting. The artist's great energy can be seen in his many portraits, still lifes, and landscapes, all of which are bursting with movement and feeling. Even though people didn't appreciate van Gogh's art during his lifetime, today he is thought to be one of the greatest artists who ever lived.

CONSTANTIN BRANCUSI (1876–1957), *pp. 24–25*

This sculptor was born in Romania and moved to Paris, France, in the early part of this century. Shortly after he arrived he was invited to be the apprentice of the great sculptor Auguste Rodin. Although many sculptors would have jumped at the chance to work with the great master, Brancusi (pronounced *bran-COOSH*) politely refused, saying "nothing grows under the shade of great trees." Working alone, Brancusi went on to become one of the most original sculptors of the twentieth century, making simple and beautiful forms of birds, fish, and people in a variety of materials, such as wood, marble, and metal.

GEORGIA O'KEEFFE (1887–1986), *pp. 26–27*

When the American Painter Georgia O'Keeffe was twelve years old, she told a friend that she would become an artist. She went to art school and later became a teacher. When she was twenty-five years old, she sent some of her watercolor paintings to her best friend, who showed them to a gallery owner in New York City. The gallery owner was Alfred Stieglitz, a very famous photographer who later became her husband. Stieglitz was so impressed with O'Keeffe's pictures that he hung them in his gallery without even asking her permission! That was the start of her long and amazing career as an artist. Her paintings show ordinary things in unusual ways, such as a single flower that fills up the whole canvas, sun-bleached animal skulls, seashells, and desert hillsides.

HENRI ROUSSEAU (1844–1910), *pp. 28–29*

This French painter decided to become a full-time artist at the age of twenty-two, at a time when art was beginning to move in a brand new direction. Rousseau (pronounced *roo-SOH*) didn't study at the important art schools of the day, called academies, but taught himself to paint and created his own special style. He liked to paint out of doors and visited zoos and gardens to get ideas for his work. Some of these ideas can be seen in his lush jungle landscapes, which are filled with exotic plants and trees, and animals that peer out from behind the thick, green foliage. This "primitive" painter's style is one of the most original in all of modern art.

JOHN SINGER SARGENT (1856–1925), *pp. 30–31*

As a boy this American painter traveled throughout Europe. He finally settled down in England, where he became an extremely popular portrait painter. Many famous and important people had their portrait painted by him. He applied paint in strong, free brush strokes, and he had a great ability to capture the feelings and personality of his sitters. Toward the end of his life he grew tired of painting portraits and switched to painting beautiful watercolors of the outdoors.

ROBERT JEW (BORN 1963), *pp. 32–33*

Robert Jew has been drawing for as long as he can remember. When he was six years old, his painting of a rabbit won a first-place ribbon in his kindergarten class, and he has been making pictures of animals and winning awards ever since. He went on to study illustration at an art college in California, and graduated "with distinction." His beautiful acrylic paintings, like the one in this book, have appeared in many advertisements and articles, and on the covers of national magazines. Today this talented illustrator teaches art and lives with his wife, three dogs, and an ever-growing menagerie of exotic lizards and "overgrown" tropical fish.

HSIANG SHENG-MO (1597–1658), *pp. 34–35*

This Chinese painter was the son and grandson of painters, and grew up surrounded by a large collection of art. Hsiang (pronounced *see-ong*) decided early in life to become an artist. He had to practice his painting at night because his father forced him to do his schoolwork during the day. He learned his craft by copying the art in his family's collection and by studying what he saw in nature. This Chinese "master" is known for his hand-scroll landscapes of rugged hillsides and mystical forests.

SUGGESTIONS FOR FURTHER READING

The following children's titles are excellent sources for learning more about the artists profiled in this book:

FOR EARLY READERS (AGES 4–7)

Venezia, Mike. *Paul Klee.* Getting to Know the World's Greatest Artists series. Chicago: Children's Press, 1991.
This easy-to-read biography combines color reproductions and humorous illustrations to capture the personality and style of this unique modern artist.

FOR INTERMEDIATE READERS (AGES 8–10)

Dubelaar, Thea, and Ruud Bruijn. *Looking for Vincent.* New York: Checkerboard Press, 1992.
A boy and his eccentric aunt go on a quest to purchase a painting by Vincent van Gogh, and in the process learn about this artist's extraordinary life.

Grosjean, Didier, and Claudine Roland. *Rousseau: Still Voyages.* Art for Children series. New York: Chelsea House Publishers, 1989.
The eccentric French artist "narrates" this clever, engaging biography. Other books in this series include: *Van Gogh: The Touch of Yellow* by Jacqueline Loumaye, 1993, and *Matisse: Painter of the Essential* by Yolande Baillet, 1993.

Paint and Painting. Voyages of Discovery series. New York: Scholastic Inc., 1994.
The history and techniques of painting are described in this beautifully designed, interactive book.

Raboff, Ernest. *Henri Matisse.* Art for Children series. New York: HarperCollins, 1988.
This informative book describes the life, times, and style of this innovative French artist. Other titles in the series are: *Vincent van Gogh, Paul Klee,* and *Henri Rousseau.*

Walker, Lou Ann. *Roy Lichtenstein: The Artist at Work.* New York: Lodestar Books, 1994.
This book examines the style and artistic process of the Pop artist, and features easy-to-read text, color reproductions, and photographs of the artist at work.

FOR ADVANCED READERS (AGES 11+)

Mühlberger, Richard. *What Makes a Van Gogh a Van Gogh.* New York: The Metropolitan Museum of Art and Viking, 1994.
Through a presentation of the Dutch painter's most memorable works, readers are shown how to recognize the artist's unique style.

Roop, Peter, and Connie Roop, ed. *Capturing Nature: The Writings and Art of John James Audubon.* New York: Walker and Company, 1993.
This book presents Audubon's life and work through his artwork and writings.

Turner, Robyn Montana. *Georgia O'Keeffe.* Portraits of Women Artists for Children series. Boston: Little, Brown and Company, 1991.
The fascinating story of O'Keeffe's life is told and illustrated with many of her most well-known paintings.

WHERE TO SEE THE ARTISTS' WORK

JOHN JAMES AUDUBON

- The New-York Historical Society
- State Historical Society of Missouri, Columbia
- Sunrise Art Museum/Fine Art Museum, Charleston, West Virginia
- Terra Museum of American Art, Chicago
- National Gallery of Art, Washington, D. C.
- Neue Nationalgalerie, Berlin
- Oklahoma City Art Museum
- Stamford Museum and Nature Center/Leonhardt Galleries, Stamford, Connecticut
- University of Rochester Art Gallery, Rochester, New York

CONSTANTIN BRANCUSI

- The Art Institute of Chicago
- Centre National d'Art et de Culture Georges Pompidou, Paris
- Dallas Museum of Art
- Museum of Art, Bucharest, Romania
- Museum of Modern Art, New York
- Philadelphia Museum of Art
- Sheldon Memorial Art Gallery, University of Nebraska, Lincoln

ALEXANDER CALDER

- Fort Wayne Museum of Art, Fort Wayne, Indiana
- Freeport Art Museum and Cultural Center, Freeport, Illinois
- Hirshhorn Museum and Sculpture Garden, Smithsonian Institution, Washington, D.C.
- Moderna Museet, Stockholm
- Museum of Fine Arts, Springfield, Massachusetts

KISHI GANKU

- British Museum, London
- Kyoto Imperial University Museum
- Los Angeles County Museum of Art
- The Metropolitan Museum of Art, New York
- Arthur M. Sackler Gallery, Smithsonian Institution, Washington, D.C.
- Tokyo National Museum

PAUL KLEE

- The Art Institute of Chicago
- Solomon R. Guggenheim Museum, New York
- Klee Foundation, Bern
- Los Angeles County Museum of Art
- Museum of Modern Art, New York
- National Gallery of Canada, Ottawa
- Philadelphia Museum of Art
- The Phillips Collection, Washington, D. C.

ROY LICHTENSTEIN

- Guild Hall Museum, East Hampton, New York
- Solomon R. Guggenheim Museum, New York
- Florida State University Gallery and Museum, Tallahassee
- Museum of Modern Art, New York
- The Whitney Museum of American Art, New York
- Stanford University Museum of Art and T.W. Stanford Art Gallery, Stanford, California
- Plattsburgh Art Museum, State University of New York, Plattsburgh

FRANZ MARC

- Bayerische Staatsgemäldesammlungen, Munich
- Solomon R. Guggenheim Museum, New York
- Museum of Modern Art, New York
- Walker Art Center, Minneapolis

HENRI MATISSE

- Albright-Knox Art Gallery, Buffalo
- The Art Institute of Chicago
- Centre National d'Art et de Culture Georges Pompidou, Paris
- Chapel of the Rosary of the Dominican Nuns, Vence, France
- The Hermitage Museum, St. Petersburg, Russia
- The Metropolitan Museum of Art, New York
- Minneapolis Institute of Arts
- Moderna Museet, Stockholm
- Musée Matisse, Nice, France
- Museum of Fine Arts, Boston
- Museum of Modern Art, New York
- Norton Simon Museum, Pasadena, California
- The Phillips Collection, Washington, D. C.
- Pushkin Museum of Fine Arts, Moscow
- Statens Museum for Kunst, Copenhagen
- Tate Gallery, London
- Wight Art Gallery Complex, University of Los Angeles

GEORGIA O'KEEFFE

- Albuquerque Museum of Art, History, and Science, Albuquerque, New Mexico
- Amon Carter Museum, Fort Worth
- Birmingham Museum of Art, Birmingham, Alabama
- Brooklyn Museum, New York
- Maier Museum of Art, Randolph-Macon Women's College, Lynchburg, Virginia
- Museum of Fine Arts, St. Petersburg, Florida
- National Museum of Women in the Arts, Washington, D. C.
- New Jersey State Museum, Trenton
- The Phillips Collection, Washington, D. C.
- Phoenix Art Museum
- Reynolda House Museum of American Art, Winston-Salem, North Carolina
- Carl Van Vechten Gallery of Fine Arts, Fisk University, Nashville

HENRI ROUSSEAU

- Musée d'Orsay, Paris
- Museum of Modern Art, New York
- Philadelphia Museum of Art
- National Gallery, Prague

HSIANG SHENG-MO

- Freer Gallery of Art, Smithsonian Institution, Washington, D.C.
- Los Angeles County Museum of Art
- The Metropolitan Museum of Art, New York
- National Palace Museum, Taipei
- Arthur M. Sackler Gallery, Smithsonian Institution, Washington, D.C.

JOHN SINGER SARGENT

- Ashmolean Museum, Oxford
- Corcoran Gallery of Art, Washington, D. C.
- Dallas Museum of Art
- M. H. de Young Memorial Museum, San Francisco
- Freer Gallery of Art, Smithsonian Institution, Washington, D. C.
- Charles and Emma Frye Art Museum, Seattle
- High Museum of Art, Atlanta
- The Metropolitan Museum of Art, New York
- Museum of Fine Arts, Boston
- Taft Museum, Cincinnati
- Tate Gallery, London
- Terra Museum of American Art, Chicago

VINCENT VAN GOGH

- The Art Institute of Chicago
- The John Paul Getty Museum, Santa Monica, California
- Solomon R. Guggenheim Museum, New York
- The Metropolitan Museum of Art, New York
- Musée d'Orsay, Paris
- Museum of Modern Art, New York
- National Gallery of Art, Washington, D. C.
- National Museum Vincent van Gogh, Amsterdam
- Rijksmuseum Kröller-Müller, Otterlo, Netherlands
- Saint Louis Art Museum
- Norton Simon Museum of Art, Pasadena, California

N. C. WYETH

- Brandywine River Museum, Chadds Ford, Pennsylvania
- Buffalo Bill Historical Center, Cody, Wyoming
- Eiteljorg Museum of American Indian and Western Art, Indianapolis
- William A. Farnsworth Library and Art Museum, Rockland, Maine
- Charles and Emma Frye Art Museum, Seattle
- Reading Public Museum and Art Gallery, Reading, Pennsylvania

CREDITS *(listed in order of appearance)*

Group of Stags c. 15,000–10,000 B.C. Mineral pigment on limestone. Lascaux Caves, Perigord, Dordogne, France. Art Resource/NY. Franz Marc (1880–1916). *The Yellow Cow,* 1911. Oil on canvas, $55\frac{3}{8} \times 74\frac{1}{2}$ in. (141×189 cm), Solomon R. Guggenheim Museum, New York. A.K.G., Berlin/Superstock. Kishi Ganku (1756–1838). *Tiger by a Torrent,* 1795. Hanging scroll, ink and color on silk. $66\frac{1}{2} \times 45$ in. (169×114.3 cm), © British Museum. N. C. Wyeth (1882–1945). *The Water Hole,* c. 1924. Oil on canvas, 28×36 in. (71.1×91.4 cm), photograph courtesy of First Interstate Bank Arizona, Phoenix. Henri Matisse (1869–1954). *The Goldfish Bowl,* 1912. Oil on canvas, $57\frac{1}{2} \times 38\frac{1}{8}$ in. (146×97 cm), Pushkin Museum of Fine Arts, Moscow. © 1995 Succession H. Matisse, Paris/Artists Rights Society (ARS), New York. Bridgeman Art Library, London/ Superstock. Roy Lichtenstein (born 1923). *Goldfish Bowl, II,* 1978. Painted and patinated bronze, $39 \times 25\frac{1}{4} \times 11\frac{1}{4}$ in. ($99.1 \times 64.1 \times 28.6$ cm), © Roy Lichtenstein. Alexander Calder (1898–1976). *Fish* (Mobile), 1940. Glass, metal wire, and cord, $16\frac{1}{4} \times 46 \times 3$ in. ($41.3 \times 116.8 \times 7.6$ cm), Hirshhorn Museum and Sculpture Garden, Smithsonian Institution, Washington, D.C.; Gift of Joseph H. Hirshhorn, 1966. © 1995 Artists Rights Society (ARS), New York/ADAGP, Paris. Paul Klee (1879–1940). *Fish Magic,* 1925. Oil on canvas mounted on board. $30\frac{3}{8} \times 38\frac{1}{2}$ in. (77.2×97.8 cm), Philadelphia Museum of Art; The Louise and Walter Arensberg Collection. © 1995 Artists Rights Society (ARS), New York/VG Bild-Kunst, Bonn. John James Audubon (1785–1851). *American Flamingo,* 1838. Hand-colored engraving with aquatint, 38×66 in. (97×66 cm). Vincent van Gogh (1853–1890). *Wheatfield with Crows,* 1890. Oil on canvas, $19\frac{7}{8} \times 39\frac{1}{2}$ in. (50.5×100.3 cm), Van Gogh Museum, Amsterdam, The Netherlands. Art Resource/New York. Constantin Brancusi (1876–1957). *Bird in Space,* 1928. Polished bronze on marble cylinder, $50\frac{1}{4} \times 17\frac{3}{4}$ in. (127.6×45.1 cm), Philadelphia Museum of Art. The Louise and Walter Arensberg Collection. © 1995 Artists Rights Society (ARS), New York/ADAGP, Paris. Georgia O'Keeffe (1887–1986). *Black Bird over Snow-Covered Red Hills,* 1946. Oil on canvas, 36×48 in. (91.4×121.9 cm), © 1995 The Georgia O'Keeffe Foundation/Artists Rights Society (ARS), New York. Photo © 1995 Malcolm Varon, N.Y.C. Henri Rousseau (1844–1910). *The Snake Charmer,* 1907. Oil on canvas, $66\frac{1}{2} \times 74\frac{3}{8}$ in. (169×189 cm), Musée d'Orsay, Paris. John Singer Sargent (1856–1925). *Crocodiles,* undated. Watercolor on paper, $15\frac{3}{4} \times 20\frac{7}{8}$ in. (40×53 cm), The Metropolitan Museum of Art, New York; Gift of Mrs. Francis Ormond, 1950. Robert Jew (born 1963). *Lizard Head,* 1994. Acrylic on canvas, 40×36 in. (101.6×91.4 cm), © Robert Jew. Hsiang Sheng-mo (1597–1658). *Frog on a Lotus Leaf* (from an album of eight leaves), 1639. Ink and color on paper, $11\frac{1}{8} \times 8\frac{3}{4}$ in. (28.3×22.2 cm), The Metropolitan Museum of Art, New York; Edward Elliott Family Collection. Purchase, The Dillon Fund Gift, 1981.